Within

ASHANTI ELAN

outskirts press

Within

v3.0

Outskirts Press, Inc.
http://www.outskirtspress.com

ISBN: 978-1-9772-2910-6

PRINTED IN THE UNITED STATES OF AMERICA

This book is dedicated to my son and daughter, please do not allow my past to determine your future. I pray that you two will shine as brightly as a millions stars in sky. I want to thank you for being a constant mirror to me, and for your patience and understanding during the ups and downs in our lives. We have been parent and child, but we have also been teacher and student to each other, and for that, I will be forever grateful to you two. My intention for writing this book is to be an example for you two, and others that are suffering with overcoming emotional and childhood traumas in order to heal and begin to live from Within.

Ashanti

Table of Contents

Preface

In 2016 my life as I knew it fell apart. I know most of you are thinking nobody's life just falls apart, and some of you know exactly what I mean because you have had a similar experience in your own life. I now know that the disruption in my life was divinely guided, it was God, our creator, shaking up my life trying to get my attention so that I could heal the broken pieces of myself and transform into the emotionally whole and balanced spiritual being that I was created to be. In order for me to transform my life, I had to go within and heal the broken and scattered pieces of myself.

Going within is a life changing tool that is a necessary component to healing what is causing the break downs in our lives. Going within is equivalent to taking a flashlight and examining those dark hidden shadow aspects of ourselves that are keeping us stuck, emotionally blocked and miserable. We have to examine those things that are causing the fear and anxiety within us. Most of us have forgotten about these traumas and have buried them deeply into our subconscious mind and now they live in our bodies and consciousness. Your shadow self is not your enemy, you do not need to get rid of it, but you do need to examine it and control it, instead of letting it control you.

In this book, I will share pieces of my spiritual journey and how I learned how to go within, and clear up some emotional and spiritual baggage in order to discover who I truly am. Through sharing my journey, I set the highest intention for you to gain the tools to maintain your energy, balance your emotions, and find the path back to your true divine self that lives within. Within you, within me, within all of humanity.

1

What Did I Miss?

In 2016, I was living what I thought to be my best life. I was working at my dream job and living in my dream home. I had two healthy, beautiful adult children, who I had raised as a single parent. It was rough at times, and I was by no means a perfect parent, but I was always willing to learn through patience, endurance and understanding, which was difficult for me because my heart was guarded and closed. I did not really know how to properly love or what love really looked like because everyone around me was afraid of it. My mother had a childlike spirit who often used money to show love. My father was just emotionally unavailable.

My intentions were to raise my children to be individuals and to stand up for themselves in the face of any type of adversity. I taught them to never let anyone take advantage of them or manipulate them into anything. I learned early in my life that you had to have tough skin and stand up for yourself in order to survive in this world because if you didn't, people will try to turn you into their puppet. I would often tell my children that if they did not have a plan for themselves, someone else would.

I am sure that I am not the only parent that has tried to push their own agendas and beliefs onto their children. It was the demise of these ideals, beliefs and agendas, that forced me to go within and examine my life as I knew it. I had to really examine every aspect of my life, beliefs, relationships and the way I was showing up in the world including my shadow self.

One Sunday I was watching an episode of Super Soul Sunday when I heard Oprah Winfrey say that your personality is supposed to represent your soul/spirit and who you are at your core, not your traumas, insecurities, ego and fears. That was my first lightbulb moment, as she calls them, and in that moment I realized that I had not been properly taught how to maximize my life and live from the inside out.

In the spring of 2016, I began to have a mental, emotional, and physical breakdown. I think, it initially started two years prior in 2014, but I thought I just needed a vacation and some rest. One day I was sitting at my desk when I was summoned into my supervisor's office and told that someone else was getting the promotion that I thought I deserved. I believed I deserved it because, I had started at the bottom and worked my way up the food chain in the company, and I had seniority in my department. The person who received the promotion was a family friend of our employer and I did not believe it was a fair and just decision.

I was livid. My feelings were hurt, I felt betrayed and invisible and I was tired of fighting these people for a spot at their table. I expressed to my supervisor how I felt, and his response let me know that he had anticipated that I would respond in this way. I stormed out of his office and told everyone that would listen about the injustice that had been done to me.

It was the first time I had personally encountered racism,

sexism, and cultural privilege, and it threw me for a loop. In the moment, I wanted to draw someone's' blood! I had been a dedicated employee of this company for almost ten years. As I think about it now, it is quite comical, but at the time I could have committed a homicide.

Things became extremely uncomfortable and difficult for me at work. Mostly because of my bad attitude and hurt feelings. I was being exceedingly difficult to work with. In my mind, I was in a war. I was in a war with my employer, war with myself, I was at war with life as a whole. Eventually, my negative attitude infected my entire life like a virus, and everything began to fall apart.

My life as I knew it started to crumble into a million little pieces. Everything I had worked for had slowly started to slip away. First my job, then my car and eventually my home. In the words of the gospel singer Shirley Caesar, "you name it!" it was all gone. I was self-sabotaging every area of my life, I became bitter and I ended up destroying a life that I had spent fifteen years and a lot of blood, sweat and tears building.

In my determination not to fail in life, I had lost myself. My life had been reduced to trying to climb a corporate ladder and being validated by people that did not give a shit about me. It was time for me to get the hell off this ladder and validate myself. The whole situation was a much-needed wake up call.

I had to question myself to figure out why I was willing to be treated this way. Was I committed to the struggle? Why did I still see myself as that unwed single teen mom, who had dropped out of high school and was placed in a juvenile detention center after all the hard work I had done to build my life. Why was I still carrying the shame of the wrong choices I had made in my past?

I still carried the shame of all those failures, with me in

my spirit. There was a voice inside of my head that constantly reminded me of every failure I have ever had, every missed opportunity, and every injustice I had experienced in my life, and that song was playing in my head on repeat.

That voice has always been a blessing and a curse to me. The blessing was that it kept me striving and pushing to do better and to be a better person even when I felt tired and defeated and wanted to give up. The curse was that it made me feel insecure and that caused me to have low self-esteem about my flaws and lately I was having a hard time controlling all of these emotions.

On the outside, it appeared that I had my life together, I think I actually believed that myself, but the cracks in my foundation was beginning to show. I was starting to feel like this was all some type of an illusion. None the less, it was an illusion I was ready and willing to maintain for the sake of appearances.

The shame and regrets made me keep pushing myself. I was juggling work, school, children, and my social life because I did not understand having balance at the time. I wanted to be an attorney. It was something I had wanted since I was a little girl.

When I was a child, my mother, would often say to me, "I hope you become a lawyer, the way you like to argue." For the record, I liked to debate not argue. I always thought arguing was pointless, no one is really listening in an argument. I just wanted to be heard, respected and understood.

My needing and wanting to be heard by people became a repetitive theme in my life, which I now understand stemmed from my childhood and family patterns. At the time, I processed it as, guarding myself and not letting anybody take advantage of me. I was closed off until I was sure the situation was safe. I was raised in a generation when children were to be seen and not heard, but I always had something to say, and I was going to say it. I learned early-on that some of the adults in my life could not be trusted.

At an early age I became a pseudo bodyguard for the less outspoken. I never hesitated to step in and speak up against any type of injustice regardless if the ill treatment was coming from a child or an adult. My aunt thought my behavior was hilarious, she started calling me by the nickname "Missy." When Missy got involved in a situation, people had better be ready to hear some hard truths and back off. Sometimes I would go too far and say too much and land myself in trouble, but I knew my grandmother would protect me from any consequences.

This behavior caused me to begin to have codependent relationships with people. See, what I thought was helping people, was actually crippling them and distracting me from my own issues. I would just swoop in, assess the situation and immediately try to come up with a solution for the problem. By doing that, I was blocking people from their chance to work through their own obstacles and relationships on their journey. I took on this sort of fixer role in my family that was toxic and a confusing reversal of the family dynamic.

This also became a reoccurring theme in my life. I would spend too much time and energy trying to solve other people's problems that my life would begin to suffer. I would become mentally, emotionally, and physically exhausted at times trying to be of service to others. I did not understand why I got so tired and drained at times. I would handle it by withdrawing from people and isolating myself. I had no idea what I was experiencing until the most codependent person in my life, my mother had died.

After my mother's death, I disconnected from my feelings. I abandoned myself so that I could hold it together for my siblings. I did not allow myself to properly grieve. This process of self-abandonment started when I first found out that my mother was sick. I began the process of shutting down my emotions so I could be strong for her and keep moving forward.

I did not think I had the luxury of checking out to deal with my feelings of loss and grief, so I pushed my feelings of grief deep down within to deal with at another time, another day, any other time than the present day. I needed to focus on getting back to my life, so I told myself, people die, that's life.

The problem with the decision to not honor what I was feeling was that, it created traumas in my subconscious. These traumas caused me to become fearful and full of anxiety. I had no idea traumas lived within us. I had no idea what traumas were or how to deal with them and work through them even if I did know what they were. Honoring what I was feeling was freighting, and since I had no idea how to do it, I would just focus on something else.

What started to happen was, all those traumas, thoughts and fears, significant or insignificant, that I thought I had stuffed deep down inside was not really buried that deep. They were actually sitting right underneath the surface, bubbling waiting to explode. Without my permission these traumas started to manifest and wreak havoc in my life.

All of my deepest and darkest fears began to unfold in my dream state at first, then into my conscious life like a tidal wave, and I was out there without a boat, raft, or even a life jacket and definitely no one to save me. The nightmares did not allow me to get any sleep. This forced me to start examining these issues so I could begin to put everything into the proper perspective.

What did I miss? What misstep had I taken, how did I get here, was all I could think about, this is where my spiritual journey began. I had to hit the pause button on my life and start to ask myself the hard but necessary questions. My first question was, who was I? I knew who I thought I was, who I wanted to be, but that was all starting to change and shift in a way that was disturbing and confusing to me.

The second question I asked myself was, why am I here on this earth, at this time. What does all this really mean because I was starting to feel out of place. It was like out of nowhere, something or someone had blindfolded me and spun me around and now I was trying to find my way back to some place I was not even sure I wanted to return to.

Feeling lost was more frightening to me than the traumas I had buried. The traumas were events that had happened to me over a long period of time. But feeling lost required immediate action. I needed to do a complete examination of my life and I was petrified just thinking about it.

I had a lot of questions, but I was not even close to having any of the answers I needed. I knew I needed clear concise answers to these questions before I could proceed with rebuilding my life and relationships. I was a lost soul trying to survive and be seen and heard in my family and in society, and that is not a place you can build healthy relationship foundations from. I needed to heal and build a healthy relationship with myself first. I needed to know who I was looking at when I looked in the mirror. Who is this person staring back at me? It was as if my soul was daring me to snatch back the curtain and come inside.

I did not recognize this person I had become now that I was taking a second look at myself, and re-examining who is behind my eyes. I also really wanted to know who was behind that annoying voice in my head that would not shut up. I started to weigh my options; I knew I could not keep this façade up. I needed a break; I was starting to have difficulties thinking straight and keeping my thoughts together. My mind was playing tricks on me, I could no longer prolong this deep spiritual work that I had to do, or burry anything else to deal with later, it had to be now. It was time to go Within.

I needed to be still. I could no longer worry about anything outside of myself. I took a six week leave of absence from work. One thing that was absolutely clear, staying at my job well past when I should have left, was a bad investment on my part. I felt like they had received way more than they deserved, or had payed me for, but I was a willing participant, so I could not put all of the blame on them. Blame was no longer going to help me anyway; it was a moot waste of time.

I went back and forth with myself for about two weeks about what my next step should be. Even though I did not have the burden of going to work every day, I was still not healing. In fact, I was getting worse because I had too much time on my hands to think and re-hash all of my issues with no knowledge of how to resolve them, and I started sinking deeper into a depressive state. I had no idea I was so full of anxiety because I had no idea what anxiety was. What I did know was that my psyche and emotions were shot to hell.

I could hardly get out of bed. I was not eating or sleeping, all I could do was cry. I was emotionally, physically, and mentally, off balance. I was abusing alcohol and marijuana to cope. I could not even watch a television show without getting emotional and crying.

After about two weeks of wallowing in self-pity, I decided this rock and roll lifestyle is not going to work for me either. I only had a limited amount of time to be on disability before I had to return to work, and I was nowhere near healed. I could not just pick up where I left off like nothing ever happened. I needed to deal with my traumas or things were going to continue to get worse for me.

I was approaching 40, what I considered to be the second half of my life and I became determined to get back on track. I refused to just lay down and die. This is not the legacy I wanted to leave behind. This is not what I worked my ass off to end up settling for. It was time to get serious about my healing.

This breakdown made me think of the times when I would interact with ill-tempered clients at work, and they would exhibit less than favorable communication or behavior, I would ask myself, what in the hell is wrong with this person? Now I understand that that person was probably traumatized by traumatic events that had happened in their life and they were in survival mode. I am sure they were plagued by their unrealized dreams, shame, fear and defeat as well, and I did not want to end up being that angry person for the rest of my life. Society is so quick to put labels on people and generalize people with emotional setbacks as being "cray." I disagree, I think most people are spiritually disconnected and lost. We have been taught that how we feel does not matter, and eventually we shut down our emotions and become numb. As a matter of fact, I knew these people, I use to be one of these people, I was related to these people, and most of them are good people once you peel back a couple of layers, but I did not want that to be my legacy.

I did not want to be reduced from being someone who could have had a life full of abundance, joy, happiness, love, and wealth to someone who had checked out when things got tuff and did not go my way. I refuse to accept defeat. I could weather another storm and get my life back on track. If this were happening to someone else, I would have been able to come up with the answers to help them. I had to give myself permission to take care of myself now. I needed to focus on me, the current state of my life and what I wanted my future to look like.

This was the turning point that I needed. I needed my own permission, and the strength to get up, dust myself off and take some action toward my healing. I acknowledged that I could not do this alone. I had to find the proper help, the only thing me and the people around me knew how to do was burry traumas in order to keep moving forward and that was toxic and unhealthy.

I needed to find someone that did not burry their traumas so that they could teach me how to stop burying mine and deal with them. My bags had gotten pretty heavy with traumas, fear, shame, anxiety, and now depression and I could not keep carrying this baggage around with me. It was time to unpack all of my baggage and I was scared as shit, because I knew what this meant. I had to go to therapy.

I was not against therapy, I just never thought I would have needed it. I did not know anyone else that went to therapy so I could not ask any questions before I decided to go. I was the one known for fixing other peoples' problems, I thought I was the therapist. All I was, was stuck in a rut lying to myself, betraying myself and dishonoring myself. I was ignoring my feelings for the sake of getting along and fitting in. I no longer cared about getting along or fitting in, I wanted to get better.

I was tired of living in fear and being a slave to my own emotions. My feelings of fear, shame and guilt needed to be tackled first. It was time to learn how to unpack all of this baggage I had accumulated and was holding on to. It was time to unpack my emotional baggage. I had never examined my emotions before, and this frightened me.

2

Unpacking

UNPACKING WAS ONE of the hardest, scariest, and demanding things I ever had to do. The first thing I did was start looking for a therapist. I did not have a clue as to how to unpack my life traumas, all I knew how to do was dwell and worry, so I started praying constantly for healing and guidance. Some days I prayed so hard and for so long, that I would end up laying on the floor for hours staring at the ceiling and talking to GOD.

I scheduled an appointment to see my primary doctor, it was actually her idea for me to take some time off from work. After reviewing my chart with me and letting me know that whatever was going on with me was not a physical problem, she decided to share a piece of her life's journey with me. She told me that after her father had passed away, she had similar symptoms and she was referred to a therapist to help her deal with her grief and fix the broken pieces of herself. When I got home that afternoon, I felt hopeful. I no longer felt alone, or like I was the only person on earth who has been through this type of breakdown in their life.

The following day I started to call some of the therapist

from the list my doctor had given me, but I was not successful in making an appointment. A week or so later I was led to a wonderful therapist named Dr. Michael. Dr. Michael was not at all what I expected a therapist to look like or behave like. Dr. Michael was a handsome, very stylish man in his mid to late fifties with kind baby blue eyes and the patience of a fisherman, he also had a quiet strength about him that never needed explaining. I was a little on edge when I first met him because the first therapist that I had met with was not a match, and we both knew it. As I was gathering my things to storm out of her office, upset that I had wasted my time going there expecting help, she asked me to follow her upstairs. She told me to have a seat, and then she disappeared like a ghost.

A few minutes later Dr. Michael walked up to me and introduced himself and asked me to follow him. We ended up in a room with about five other people sitting in a circle. I quickly scanned the room as I sat down making sure I did not recognize anybody and also thinking, I know this man did not think I was about to sign up for no damn group therapy. I was not willing to share my personal business with a bunch of strangers. No way, not going to happen in a million years.

Just as I was about to stand up, and just walk out, Dr. Michael sat down in the chair next to me, closest to the exit door. He gently placed his hand on my shoulder and told me to relax. He said, you can put your things down they will be safe. I had not realized how tightly I was holding onto my coat and purse until he had said something. We both chuckled and I complied to his request. He asked me to give it a chance and he stood up and walked away to begin the session.

As I sat there listening to other people's stories about their heartbreaks, injustices, shame and guilt, I started to connect with them through empathy. Empathy allowed me to stop focusing on my pain and support someone else in getting through theirs. When it was my turn to share, I was almost shaking with fear, but I mustered up the strength to start talking. It felt like I was having an out of body experience. I knew it was me talking, but I felt like I was standing next to myself just observing the whole thing. As I was talking, I experienced a flood gate of emotions and feelings that I have not felt in years come rushing in. I cried a bucket of tears that day, and it felt good to just finally let it all out.

When I got home that afternoon, I felt better, lighter even, and hopeful that this might be a good thing for me. Not just so I could go back to work or deal with my mother's death. I decided that I was going to give therapy a real chance. It was a six-week program, with a minimum of two to three meetings a week. I readily signed the contract and was eager to get to work on my healing.

In group, there was no judgement, no masks, no ego or pride, just raw emotions and genuine requests for love and understanding for one another's traumas. I grew to know these people better than I knew some of my own family members because they had let me in, they were willing to be vulnerable. We were all at a point in our lives where lying about what bought us here and our experiences was no longer an option. We became a family filled with love, empathy, understanding and support for one another that was genuine and felt safe.

I will only share one of my experiences in detail, because I respect the privacy of the program. This was my experience of learning and understanding what unpacking truly meant. Dr. Michael approached me halfway through the program and said to me, I want you to try something, I said ok. What is it? He said, I want you to have a conversation with yourself. I replied, what exactly do you mean? He took two chairs and faced them toward each other.

He went on to say, I want you to ask yourself a question in one chair, and I want you to answer your question in the other chair. I turned around and looked at Dr. Michael like he was the one that needed therapy. He just smiled and waited for me to accept the challenge. I closed my eyes for a moment, as I reopened them, I looked around the room, and what I saw were the eyes of everyone else staring at me lovingly waiting for my response. That was enough for me to say ok, I will do it.

I took a deep breath and grabbed a box of tissues from the table and sat down in one of the chairs. I can remember being so scared, this was a whole other level of being vulnerable. I desperately wanted to heal, but at the same time, I was afraid of what would come up during this healing experiment. I trusted Dr. Michael and the group to support me, now I needed to trust myself and the process.

At this point, I had already shared with everyone in the group what happened to me at work and my feelings about my mother dying, but not my deepest darkest fears that had been chasing and controlling me since childhood. Now I was being presented with the opportunity to speak to that child within face to face. It was time to have a chat with Missy as my aunt called her. She was the little girl inside of me that held onto all of my childhood pain and traumas. It was time for Missy to speak her peace and finally be heard, validated and supported. I was not going to let Missy ruin my life because she was still hurting. She needed the compassion, empathy, love and understanding now that eluded her as a child.

There would be no one telling her to be quiet, do not cry, you cannot say that, that is rude, or you are wrong for feeling that way, you guys know what I am talking about. There was no one telling her that it is not okay to be yourself and looking at me sideways when I am considered to be stepping out of line. None of that energy was there. I had free range to just say whatever I wanted. I yelled, screamed and even threw the box of tissues at the other part of my-self that had let Missy down in the past. The part of myself that allowed people to use, abuse and betray her had been called on the carpet.

Let me tell you something guys, if unpacking was the goal, I left a thirty thousand square foot mansion full of furniture in that room. I bared my soul and it felt great! I was crying so hard when I was done, I could barely see a foot in front of my face. When I was finally exhausted and did not have any tears left, I remembered there were other people in the room.

As I looked around the room and began to see all the tears of compassion streaming down their faces and the empathy in their eyes, I knew I had made the right decision to accept this challenge. It truly felt like an outer body experience. As I stood up, Dr. Michael gave me a hug and told me that I did good and to go home and rest for the rest of the day.

When I got home, I ended up laying on my bedroom floor staring at the ceiling again, thinking to myself, girl did you really just have a conversation with yourself? I answered, yes you did, and I think it just changed your life. I felt lighter and hopeful, like a Phoenix rising from the ashes of despair and this was just the beginning. If there is anyone reading this who is contemplating going to therapy but is afraid of being labeled crazy for trying to get help, I am here to tell you THAT IS COMPLETE BS! Go get help, there is no shame in wanting to be a whole and healthy person. Please do not let anyone rob you of an opportunity to heal because of their fears and ignorance of mental heal issues we all have faced at one time or another.

Consider therapy a realignment of your emotions. If we have to get the tires on our vehicles realigned after hitting too many bumps, it only makes sense that our spirit and bodies would eventually need a realignment after years of wear and tear on our emotions. Therapy is a safe space, it is an opportunity to heal from a place of willingness and self-cooperation. It is also necessary in order to begin unpacking a lifetime of emotional, mental, and physical baggage that is probably keeping you stuck and stagnant in your life.

The day I completed my therapy program was both satisfying and disappointing. I was proud of myself and my accomplishments. I felt better, my anxiety had subsided. I knew for sure I was not loco, and I was hopeful about the future, but I was going to miss Dr. Michael and my group family. I trusted them more than I trusted people I knew my whole life, but I had to keep moving forward on my journey, we all did.

We all said our goodbyes and I left with my certificate of completion in hand ready to tell everyone about my experience. Some people understood, some did not, it really did not matter to me. I knew the benefits I had received, and I also knew it was not something you could convince people to do. Either they were ready for the healing process or they were not, therapy is not something you can do for another person, healing is a solo journey.

I knew I had to check back into life. I had gotten through this difficult time in my life without the use of anti-psychotic or anti-depressant medications or alcohol and anger, and I was proud of that. I was offered medication on numerous occasions, but I needed to feel these emotions in order to heal them. One thing that was clear to me, was that I did not want my old life back and I did not want any more crutches. Go figure, I started this journey partly to get my old life back on track, now I did not even want it. It was time to put my new set of skills to work, I wanted to apply them in my life and create a new life conducive to who I am now.

3

New Perspective

Now that therapy was over, and Dr. Michael had moved on to helping others, I had to figure out what my next move was. I knew I was nowhere near being completely healed, but I was healed and open enough to keep moving forward and keep learning and growing. I wanted to rebuild my life and relationships in a positive and healthy way. I had unpacked enough internal clutter and traumas that I was able to really see deeper into myself and where my soul lies. I could start to have a mutual relationship with my true divine self. One based off of kindness and compassion. A relationship that would cultivate and represent who I really am. I am no longer just going to go with the flow, putting up with or tolerating people, places and things that no longer serve me or add any value to my existence.

The next part of my spiritual journey was church. I was not necessarily raised in a church so to speak, but I had attended on holidays. I had joined a church and gotten baptized when I was twenty-seven years old. I thought I knew how to do be a christian, but I really only knew what was expected of me in the institution.

I knew how to lay all my burdens on GOD's alter and pray for my problems to magically disappear. I remember thinking to myself one Sunday in church, why does everyone, including myself keep showing up here every week asking for the same things over and over with another add on from time to time? I asked myself, do prayers get permanently answered? Or are they bandages to give you the hope and strength to hold on until next week, because my prayers felt like they were stuck in the eithers or only partially getting answered.

In the summer of 2017, my sisters friend invited us to attend his church. It was refreshing, it felt like the perfect next step after therapy. It was exactly what I thought I needed. I had cleared up a lot of emotional baggage, now it was time for a spiritual check-up. This is where things got interesting.

In the beginning, Church was going well. I started to open up more spiritually, I also started to build bonds and friendships with people in the church. The people in the congregation were nice, they accepted my sister and I with open arms, but something within me was stopping me from becoming a member. I did not think it was wise to jump into any commitments just yet on my healing journey, but that was not the only reason.

As I was starting to open up more spiritually, I developed an obsession with the new testament, I read it over and over. I was fascinated with Jesus's life. His message was starting to become crystal clear to me. I wanted to connect with him spiritually because in the bible it says that we could, so I started talking to him constantly. I would ask him tons of questions and wait for the answers to show up in my spirit and manifest into my life through different outlets, such as television shows, movies, music and other people. I was not interested in a routine that would only make me feel good one or two days out of seven, what was I supposed to do the other five days?

I wanted to experience the everlasting love and peace within that Jesus was talking about.

I started to dissect Jesus's life and what his message was really trying to tell us and why he used so many parables. I was intrigued by the way he spoke about the Divine Holy Spirit and the messages he delivered to the people of his time about life, spirituality, love, faith, everlasting life and most importantly the knowing. The knowing of life's mysteries and secrets. The knowing that nothing is as it seems on the surface.

Most importantly, learning the power of letting go. There is no way you can ascend like Jesus being weighed down by life's imaginary obstacles. Jesus's faith in this knowing and his spirituality and trust in the Divine Holy Spirit was unwavering. He was willing to walk in his faith and be an example of what was possible even after his physical death. It got me to thinking, what would have happened if Jesus would have stayed in the temple and conformed to the status quo.

For some reason that thought scared me and gave me hope at the same time. At that point I knew I could not rely on any kind of routine or religious dogma if I wanted to follow Jesus's teaching. I had to be led by my spirit and the Divine Holy Spirit within. I needed to change my perspective about Christianity, spirituality and the proper way to heal traumas by focusing more on the knowing. I know the Divine loves me and supports me and only wants the best for me. I know that every obstacle or set back is just a set up for my healing. If there is no test, then how can we have a testimony to help others.

Everyone in church assumedly already had a personal relationship with Jesus. I wanted to be a living example to people who did not know him and had never heard or understood his true message. He did not try to convince people to follow him, or be like him, he shared the Divine's message, of love, oneness, and everlasting life by using his spiritual gifts and steady movement on his journey. He did not coddle people or treat them like children, Jesus did not play games with people or ask them for anything in return. His journey was short, but he did leave the blueprint that has been misconstrued in more ways than not. I often refer to the new testament as Jesus's memoirs.

One of the things that stood out to me while I was studying Jesus legacy was that, we all must leave our memoirs, they are blueprints for the next generation. It is the most important part of our legacy. It is the roadmap that led us to our destinies. Sadly, the only story most of us leave behind is written or told by someone else, we call them obituaries, family stories, the evening news or gossip. Do not let someone else tell your story, because it is important to society and may help someone else.

I made a conscious decision to partner up with myself, my creator, my spirit guides and my ancestors and continue on my journey. Wherever this journey leads me, I know in my heart it is my destiny. I had to throw fear in the trash and learn how to trust myself and the Divine Holy Spirit.

I do not want to give anyone the illusion of thinking your spiritual journey is going to be like riding around on a magic carpet like Aladdin with your legs crossed, thinking you're going to get a Genie in a bottle to grant all your wishes and call it GOD. The Genie on this journey is you. You are in control; you always have been, and you always will be. Stop looking outside of yourself for the answers they are within you.

This spiritual journey is going to be the hardest thing that you have ever had to face, but the rewards are priceless. All you need for this journey is a knap sack full of faith, love, understanding, forgiveness, obedience, compassion, empathy and willingness. These things you will need for sure, and if you do not have all of them now, you will definitely pick them up on your journey.

Think of Dorothy in the Wizard of Oz, when she decided to go on her journey, the yellow brick road was illuminated to her, and it was her choice whether to stay stuck in Oz or to save herself. Dorothy had to realize her destiny and ease on down the road without a clue of where she would end up. She knew where she wanted to go, but there was never any guarantee that she would get there. What showed up for Dorothy was her traumas and obstacles that were blocking her from living her best life. Are you willing to take the first step in your healing journey?

If you are, congratulations! You are about to discover who you really are at your core, and your purpose for existing on this planet at this time. This is where you start to develop the things that money cannot buy. Internal peace cannot be bought, faked, or manufactured because it comes from within. Nothing outside of you really matters on this journey except how you handled it.

Once you master the YOU that is within and balance your emotions, your life will automatically begin to transform into what it was always meant to be; you will transform into the spiritual being having a human experience that YOU were always meant to be. When I started to understand this truth, I was able to open up more to my experiences because I understood that they were only lessons followed by tests. I stopped processing my obstacles as negative nuisances and started viewing them as opportunities to heal traumas and unpack old baggage and clear blockages I did not even know existed in my life.

Here is some food for thought, God is our creator, the ultimate power, the source of all creation. GOD tells us, you can come home to source anytime you want by going within and asking for help and guidance when we are stuck, lost and confused. GOD does not exist to hold our baggage or forgive our sins. GOD uses people, places and things as our mirror and co-creator of our life experiences, good or bad. If you hurt, harm, injure and destroy one of GOD's other creations, then that is what you create for yourself as well. GOD will not shield you or protect you from the mess you have created, but GOD will take you by the hand and give you the opportunity to accept responsibility, take accountability for you actions, and make amends for whatever you have done.

There is no handing it over to GOD and washing your hands of it. The goal is to self-partner and heal that abused, hurt child and nurture the good parts of yourself. Nurture the good things that make children so precious, and who they really are at their core before the traumas happened in their lives. Does Missy still act up sometimes? Yes, she does, but she does not control my emotions and life anymore. Now when she shows up throwing a temper tantrum, I lovingly ask her why she is upset, so we can review, discuss, and resolve, the trauma that has triggered her, so we can lovingly release it from within. This is the Quantum ideology that helped me.

When I first started going within, there were so many fragmented parts of myself that it frightened me. I had no idea that I had split myself into so many different versions just to survive. I began with having a meet and greet with these fragmented parts of me to find out how old they were and what their traumas were. Internally, I had not emotionally matured passed the age of around sixteen. It was a rude awakening to find out that I had only matured physically, and I would have continued to be stuck at that age emotionally, spiritually, and mentally, if my life had not fallen apart.

I started with the youngest version of myself first. This version of me was a baby in my mother's womb that did not feel wanted. I have no idea what my mother was going through when she was carrying me, I only know what I felt. It is really important to your healing not to second guess the information that you receive from within. If you are really brave, you can ask your spirit to show you the experience and walk you through the trauma. I started to do this around the third time I went within because I felt like I was healed enough to not get stuck in the trauma.

Some of the things that were revealed to me brought me to my knees with hurt and pain, and some left me feeling enlightened. After I reviewed it, I was able to gain a better understanding of the choices I was making from that broken unhealed state of who I thought I was. Things were now starting to make sense to me. I felt like I was meeting myself for the first time. I had to parent myself, from an infant to the age of sixteen years old. By the time I was sixteen, I had already experienced enough trauma that I had disconnected from my emotions because I viewed them as a weakness because they were never validated by anyone.

4

Identifying Triggers & Traumas:

Have you ever gotten that paralyzing feeling in your body that stops you in your tracks or immediately angers you? It often feels like someone just lit the back of your neck on fire or punched you in the gut out of nowhere. This feeling will cause you to instantly react before thinking. It normally stems from some form of verbal communication, or information, or even an experience that triggers a negative feeling in you that causes you to react in a negative way. You either end up getting into a verbal dispute or an actual physical fight with another person, place or thing. This is called a trigger; triggers are caused by buried traumas.

Some traumas you are aware and conscious of because they are still affecting your daily life, but most of your traumas stem from your childhood and were probably buried and forgotten about. These traumas have been locked away deep into your subconscious mind because you did not possess the tools at the time to process them and move forward from the trauma in a healthy way. Most of us were children or young adults when these traumas happened. Some of us were victims of someone else reliving their traumas and insecurities at our expense, and neither of us had any idea how to process what happened or how to make it stop. This plays out in our relationships disguised as heated arguments, jealousy, survival, envy, greed, backstabbing, lying, cheating, you get the point. All of these negative emotions and behaviors come from a traumatized state and operating in survival mode.

You must first accept and understand that what happened to you as a child or as a victim of someone else, was not your fault, but unfortunately it is your responsibility to heal yourself and not let it ruin your life. Through my experiences, and learning from other people's journeys, I have learned that the negative energy caused by our traumas that we compartmentalize and burry within, takes on a life of its own, and need to be fed by our insecurities. For example, do you know someone that is not happy unless there is drama and chaos going on? They will go out of their way to be negative or to hurt someone else. That is them living out their traumas over and over again. If we do not heal these traumas, they will escalate and may cause irreversible consequences in our lives and the lives of others. We can also see how unhealed traumas connect and become one big negative consciousness that manifest into society as systematic racism, sex trafficking, corrupt government entities, and police brutality. How many more generations is America going to perpetuate the same traumas against black people?

After you learn how to self-partner with the broken and traumatized child buried within, and begin to heal, by nurturing your good qualities and all the positive things about yourself, your life will instantly start to transform in a positive way. You will no longer feed into anyone else's drama or continue re-enacting your own traumas. The triggers will no longer exist, and you will be able to walk away from a negative situation lovingly and compassionately without the need to fix anyone or make them understand anything. You can walk away peacefully because you understand that everyone is on a journey to self-discovery and some will get there faster than others.

Instead of focusing on anything that is negative, start to nurture the things that your inner child loves doing, all of the things that make you genuinely happy. You have to explore those buried parts of yourself and get more acquainted with yourself and who you really are at your core, while dismissing what other people want you to be that probably caused you some type of trauma in your life. When your inner child starts to heal, you will begin to laugh from your gut again, and smile for no particular reason other than you are alive. You will begin to spiritually mature into the strong confident person you were always meant to be and live from the inside out.

When I first started the process of going within, I was broken into a million little pieces. There would be days when I would be triggered, and I was afraid to ask myself why, because I did not know what was going to be revealed to me. Somethings that were revealed to me, I had forgotten all about, and some I did not even know affected me in way that would cause trauma. For example, seeing one of my siblings getting a beating for something they did. When I was growing up, I thought children were supposed to get beatings so they could learn right from wrong because society led us to believe that it was an acceptable form of punishment. Now, I cringe at the thought of a child getting a beating because I know they are just trying to express themselves in the only way they know how. Every trauma is not going to be one that confines you to your bed, or cause depression, but it will help you to understand yourself and where your traumas stem from.

When I had gotten to a point where I had healed about eighty percent of my childhood traumas, there was a sort of calm and internal peace coming from within that came over me. I was no longer so sensitive and insecure about the traumas that I had endured. I was now able to honestly speak about them and how they had affected my life consciously and unconsciously. By speaking to other people, I realized that most of us have been through a lot of the same traumas. Human beings are pretty much creatures of habit, and we all know how history loves to repeat itself for generations. One of the most important things I learned from group therapy was that, acknowledgement, accountability, processing, forgiving, and releasing is a great formula to heal emotional traumas.

It was by no means an easy choice for me to open up and be this vulnerable by sharing my traumas publicly. Healing them was one thing, but sharing them publicly is a whole other level of vulnerability that I was not sure that I was ready for, but I started to have this nagging feeling coming from within as confirmation to me that it was my duty to try and assist as many people as I could, by just simply being honest about my experiences, and how I was able to overcome my childhood traumas and become emotionally unstuck. After reviewing my journals that I had accumulated throughout my life, it dawned on me that I had been writing this book my entire life. If any of my traumas that I shared in the next section of this book helps one person or millions of people, it is worth the vulnerability and the intimacy I will share with every single reader.

5

Trauma 1: Who Am I?

1976 IS THE year I was born into this world. The first five or six years were pretty much uneventful. Around the age of six years old I started to become aware of my surroundings, the people in my life and human behaviors. I was a quiet child, the kind that did not say much, but I watched everything and everybody. I loved school and learning new things and I excelled in all subjects.

My parents had split up shortly after my younger sister was born. My sister and I was not sad about that fact. I know most children wanted their parents to stay together but not us. My parents were polar opposites. My father was extremely strict and stern in his interactions with us. My mother was very passive aggressive and just wanted to have fun. Me personally, I thought it would have been an emotional roller coaster ride and for sure and unstable family unit if they had stayed together for our benefit.

By the time my sister and I had reached Junior high school we had a pretty comfortable routine splitting our time between both of our families. As I am writing this and reflecting back, it was very balanced, we were happy but mischievous children that spent and equal amount of time with both sides of our families and we had a stepfather that treated us like his own children.

That all changed when my mother cheated on my stepfather and we got kicked out of our home. Our lives went downhill fast, and to be completely honest it never got much better for my mother. In 1985 my mother gave birth to my brother, I was ten and my sister was nine, and our carefree childhood started to slowly fade away. My sister and I loved and took care of our baby brother and ourselves the best that nine and ten year old's could.

By the time I reached high school, I had been through things no one should have had to endure, let alone a prepubescent teen lost in this world with no one to save me. It almost felt like one day I was a happy go lucky ten-year-old, and in a blink of an eye I turned into an emotionally unbalanced teenager looking for someone to save me from myself. Isn't that what life is supposed to be about? Saving people from themselves and their bad decisions. No one saved my mother, and they definitely did not come to save my sister and me.

That was our introduction to the trauma of loss. Yes, we were children, but we lost everything too. We loss the comfort of our home, toys, clothes, stability, pretty much everything we owned. We began to move around staying with different family members until we eventually moved into my mother's childhood home with my uncle and his wife and kids, after my grandparents decided it was time for them to downsize.

We eventually adjusted to our new life, but none of us dealt with or knew how to deal with the traumas we had just experienced. My brother's father was a kind and loving man, that my sister and I grew to love deeply. Unfortunately, he was killed in a freak accident at work before my brothers first birthday so there we were, abandoned again and left to pick up the pieces and try to move on and rebuild our lives. The problem was my mother was from an upper middle-class family and she did not really know how to handle the struggles we were facing, and the death of the love of her life almost killed her. She had too much pride to ask my grandfather for help until we were almost homeless.

My mother had an emotional breakdown after his death, which left my sister and I responsible for taking care of ourselves and my brother longer than we had anticipated. In less than two years our lives had completely changed. It changed me in ways that altered how I felt about my life, the future, and my mother. I had to learn how to survive on my own. This is when I created my alter ego Missy. Missy was not going to depend on anyone, especially a man to provide for her, or let a man ruin her life. Missy had fangs and was ready and willing to bite anybody at any time. Missy kept us safe, she cooked and cleaned and made sure our lives did not fall apart again.

Missy helped me through a lot of tuff things growing up, but she was neglected and grew to be resentful of most of the adults in my life. In order to heal I had to make peace with her, nurture her, listen to her, and validate her pain in order for her to be at peace. I spent a lot of time within working on Missy until we became one. Missy will live within me forever, but she no longer controls my thoughts and behavior. When I feel Missy trying to take over a situation, I go within and find out what is going on with her and why she is being triggered, and together we resolve the issues causing these feelings internally.

I love Missy, she is me and I am her. I appreciate everything she has done to get us to this point in our life, but I cannot live my adult life with the emotions, thoughts, and outlook on life of a ten-year old or a teenager. It was time to grow up emotionally and spiritually and learn how to balance my emotions. It was time to go within and explore the traumas of loss, abandonment, betrayal, instability, lack, and the loss of my childhood that still resided within me. Missy was tired and stuck in a time loop of reliving childhood traumas that she was not equipped to handle. Missy just wanted to be a child and it is time I let her.

6

Trauma 2: Sex

When I was thirteen years old, I got pregnant for the first time by a neighborhood boy a year or two older than I was. Both of my grandmothers told me that, if I wanted to keep the baby that it was ok with them. Everyone else was still clutching their pearls saying, "oh no, but you are so smart, you are so young, you are so quiet", all I could do was stare at them thinking, don't you think I know all of that already. I was not trying get pregnant or even have sex when it happened. How does something like this happen to someone like me? I was fighting and squirming around the whole time trying to get away from the boy on top of me trying to have sex with me only to still get pregnant.

Something told me, rather warned me, that I should not go to his house. I had a feeling that I should just go home or to the playground, but I ignored my intuition because my cousin had a crush on his friend and he was going to be there, so I changed my mind and went with her, now I'm pregnant. I immediately started thinking of ways to hide my pregnancy when I first found out. The last thing I wanted to do was tell my mother that I had gotten pregnant. I thought she would have made me keep the baby out of spite.

This is not how I imagined having sex for the first time would happen. It definitely was not the way having sex was portrayed in movies and television. I was supposed to fall in love, get married and then start a family by having sex. I was too young to be responsible for a child, and I did not have any romantic feelings for the father of my child. I just wanted to hide. I hid my pregnancy for as long as I could, but my sister told my mother, and by the end of the day, my entire family knew. I was embarrassed and humiliated, but I was glad I did not have to hide anymore.

This trauma that took less than fifteen minutes to create, gave me unhealthy ideas and views about sex and relationships for decades. I did not require love and intimacy from men before I would have sex with them because of this experience. My innocence was stolen from me, and at the time I did not even know it. I did feel violated when it was over and I fought like an alley cat trying to prevent it from happening, but I was not aware that I had been sexually assaulted at the time. I think I processed it that way because he was a child too. He was a year or two older than I was, and we had known each other almost our entire lives. We were always taught to be aware of adults trying to take advantage of children, but not how to handle being violated by another child.

I had no desire to tell an adult or call the police and report what had just happened to me. I wanted to slap him upside his head a few times, but that was it. A few years later it happened to me again by another friend. This time I understood that I had been sexually assaulted, but I still chose not to report it to the authorities because I was embarrassed and ashamed that it had happened to me again by someone I trusted. This time I told my mother, who told my aunt, who told my uncle. When my uncle got involved, it became less about what happened to me, and more about him being disrespected by someone he knew. He was irate that someone would have enough guts to violate his family in this manner.

My feelings and emotions became secondary. I felt like I had gotten swept up in a bad gangsta movie, but I was grateful that he cared enough to stand up for me, so I just agreed with what he said and let him handle it. Shortly after this happened another alter ego emerged from within me. This is when Shynedelly was created. Shynedelly was ten times meaner than Missy. Missy would just cuss you out, Shynedelly would cut you.

Shynedelly was going to make sure Missy and I were protected and would never be sexually assaulted again. She not only protected us, she also protected other people. Shynedelly vetted our friends and family before letting anyone in. She built walls tall enough that no one could get in and Missy and I could not get out. She preferred three-month relationships over true intimate genuine relationships due to the fear of being violated or hurt again. Shynedelly was a good friend, but she was a codependent people pleaser. I do no think she needed to be liked, but the people she loved and chose to let in, she would move mountains for.

Shynedelly navigated us through college, corporate America and motherhood. She was pretty calm and pleasant unless you crossed her in anyway. I became comfortable letting Shynedelly take the lead role in my life. That meant that Missy and I could stay in hiding and guard our emotions and traumas like they were hostages. This worked for about fifteen years until she got burnt out and over traumatized by life and collapsed after my mother died. Shynedelly had quit, and there was nothing I could do to make her get back into position.

7

Trauma 3: Teen Pregnancy

I WAS SICK as a dog the first two months of my pregnancy. I threw up every morning on my way to school, which made me extra hungry and cranky by the time I finally got there. I had only told one person since I found out that I was pregnant. That was my cousin who was with me the day I had gotten pregnant, but it still did not feel real to me. My cousin and I went to planned parenthood in the city so I could get examined and find out how far along I was in my pregnancy. I chose planned parenthood because I knew they would not contact my parents and tell them that I was pregnant before I was ready for them to find out.

I found out at the appointment that I was almost four months pregnant and my belly was starting to poke out. I stayed in hiding and wore oversized clothes to conceal my pregnancy. I would go straight to my bedroom after school and stay there until I could hear my mother snoring before I would sneak down to the kitchen and grab me some food. All my sneaking around came to a screeching halt after my sister went through my bookbag and found the prescription for my prenatal vitamins from the clinic and gave them to my mother. Needless to say, all hell broke loose in my house that night.

My mother only asked me two questions, the first one was, are you pregnant? I believe she asked me that question even though she was holding the proof in her hands because she was in shock. I said yes, she said by whom? I told her, but for some reason I left out the part about him strong arming me and holding me down out of my responses. I did not know it was rape or sexual assault at the time, and I was still confused and traumatized by the whole situation.

The next thing I know, my mother was on the telephone calling anyone with a telephone and ears to tell them that I was pregnant. The next morning, she woke me up early in the morning and told me to get dressed. The first stop was grand-ma's house, which was not so bad because I knew that my grandmother loved me and was not mad at me. Disappointed yes, but I was her partner in crime and her confidant. She spoke her peace to my mother and moved on busying herself in the kitchen. About an hour into the visit, the front door abruptly flew open and in rushed my aunt's boyfriend with the father of my unborn child by the collar.

My face hit the floor. I was in a state of shock and thinking what in the hell is he doing here in my grand-parents' home. I had no real interest in this boy, he had raped me, now I am pregnant, hasn't he done enough? I wanted to just cry, and scream get his ass out of here! But I did not say a word, I just watched and listened to other people make decisions about me that would affect me for the rest of my life. He and I didn't even speak to each other, but I'm sure he was more afraid than I was because if I would have told my aunts boyfriend what he really did, this situation would have cost him more than money.

I would not look directly at him; we shared a few glances but that was it. I honestly just wanted him to leave before my grandfather got home from work and walked smack dab into the middle of this mess I created. It was decided for me that I would go to New York City and have a procedure done that could not quite be called an abortion because I was too far along in my pregnancy to have an abortion. I had to go to NY because I was too far along in my pregnancy to have an abortion in Pennsylvania. In my thirteen-year-old mind, it did not sound that bad because I knew I was not ready to have a child.

When we arrived at the facility, I started to have second thoughts. Not because I wanted a child, but because the procedure sounded horrendous and it was. It still haunts my psyche to this day. It took me many years and a lot of deep spiritual healing to finally forgive myself. Even if I did speak up, what would I have said, and who would have listened to me? I was not ready to have a child; I was only thirteen years old. I did not even consider putting the baby up for adoption at the time because I was too ashamed about being pregnant. I just wanted the whole situation to go away so I could return to my life before all this happened.

8

Trauma 4: The Procedure

We left for New York City around three o'clock in the morning on the day of the procedure. My aunt and uncle were busy talking about all the things they wanted to do and buy in New York while I was getting the procedure done. I do not remember my mother having too much to say the entire trip. I was sitting in the back seat starring out of the window thinking, what in hell have I gotten myself into. Was it too late to change my mind?

I was really scarred by the time we arrived, but I knew I was too young to be having a baby for goodness sake, I am still a child myself. The only thing I could do to keep me from opening the car door and bolting down the street was the thought that this will all be over tomorrow. In a few days, I will be back in school, back hanging out with my family and friends like nothing ever happened. How is an honors student supposed to explain having a baby at thirteen years old? I did not know, nor did I want to.

When we arrived at the clinic it was dark and dreary. The walls were painted with bright colors, but the lights were dim.

It kind of felt like I was in another country because everyone that worked there was African or Jamaican and spoke with heavy accents. I vaguely remember the doctor; I do remember he was a black man with a short haircut and black glasses. After he explained the procedure and my mother signed the all the paperwork, they left, and I was alone.

The nurse that was assigned to me was a middle-aged African woman with a calm face and a gentle touch. If it were not for her, I do not know how I would have gotten through that procedure. Shortly after I arrived the doctor came into my room and inserted a white tube looking object into my vagina. When he finished, he said to me, in a couple of hours, I would start having contractions. I had no idea what a contraction felt like, but I guess I was getting ready to find out. It probably would have made more sense to me if he would have said, I will be back when you start screaming.

I fell asleep before I started having contractions because I had not slept in at least forty-eight hours. I have no idea what time it was when I was jolted awake by the worst pain I ever felt in my life. The nurse came in and just stared at me for a few moments before she grabbed my hand and started rubbing it. She said, just breathe, it will be over soon, and she left the room. When she returned, she had a portable toilet with her, but I was in too much pain to ask her what it was for.

This horrible unbearable pain lasted for several hours before she left to go get the doctor. At this point I was screaming at the top of my lungs and squirming around in pain not knowing what to do or how to make it stop. When the doctor came in, he told me to sit on the portable toilet and push. I was in too much pain to actually process what he was instructing me to do, I just did it. I do not remember how many times I pushed until the baby came out but eventually it did. I peeked between my legs because I just had to see what it was that was inside of me causing all this pain.

When it was over, the nurse laid me down on the bed and rolled the portable toilet out of the room with my first-born dead baby in it. I felt sad, confused, relieved and free all at the same time. When it was time for me to go within and heal this trauma. I kept getting this feeling of tightness in my chest that made me feel like I was having a heart attack. It was fear because it was time to face what I had done. I had to push past the fear because this trauma was holding me back from growing and maturing. I carried the shame of it every day, and to make matters worse the baby father would remind me of what I did every time I ran into him for years.

Later that day, my mother, aunt, and uncle, came back to pick me up and I was happy to leave, I was eager to get home and take a hot shower and put this all behind me. The doctor gave me a prescription for an antibiotic and a list of instructions telling me what I could and could not do. I was a little surprised that I was no longer in any real pain. I was a little sore and still bleeding, but I was able to walk to the car. No one offered me hug, or even asked me if I was feeling okay. It was as if we had gone on a normal shopping trip to New York City instead of what we had really gone there to do.

The ride back to Philadelphia was quiet. I guess they had a good time shopping and partying last night and was too tired for conversation. I stayed home from school that day, and the day after, the following day I returned to my normal routine like it never happened. I put the whole experience behind me, so I thought, and I never spoke about it again for almost 30 years. It was a traumatic experience for me, and I thought I could just forget all about it, and if enough time goes by, I could just pretend that it never happened, but that was not the case.

I had to face it to heal it and forgive myself. I was a child when it happened, but even if I was an adult at the time, I do not know if I would have been able to take care of a child that was a product of me being raped. I had to forgive my mother, she was on this journey with me and I am sure she thought it was the best decision at the time for the family as a whole. Now that I am older, I can see the big picture, I wish I would have chosen adoption and given a family that gift. This experience left me with the traumas of shame, guilt, rape, abandonment, embarrassment, and the feeling of not being enough.

When my children were born, I had a hard time connecting and bonding with them and I did not know why. I was a good provider and protector, but emotionally I was detached. This created an emotional distance between us that I was not conscious I was creating at the time. I discovered through my healing process that this behavior was connected to the traumatic experience I had with my first pregnancy. Deep down I felt like I did not deserve a child because of what I had done, and I was constantly worrying that something was going to happen to one of them, I had no peace.

9

Trauma 5: High School

I STARTED HIGH school in 1990. After everything that had happened the previous year, my family decided it would be best to send me to an all-girls catholic high school. This was probably a punishment for getting pregnant. I did not really have a problem with the new school at first, I honestly needed a change of atmosphere. When I returned to school last year after the procedure, it was hard to explain throwing up every day and gaining almost twenty pounds in four months to all of sudden slimming back down and looking normal again to a bunch of twelve- and thirteen-year-old children.

I really did not need the drama; I would rather start fresh with new people who did not know anything about me. I was a little upset about the uniforms because I loved fashion. I would spend hours at a time putting outfits together and styling my hair and now I had to dress and look like everyone else. This caused me to get more creative. I would dye my hair bright colors just so I would not blend in. The school was predominantly Caucasian and Hispanic, but I was always mistaken for being Hispanic, so I had to find another way. I have always been different, and I liked that about me, I did not follow fads or trends that was too boring for me.

The first month was spent getting to know the new program. Catholic school was a lot different than public school. The classrooms were actually quiet, the bathrooms were clean and there was no graffiti anywhere. The cafeteria was orderly, the food was good, and the hallways were spotless. Our uniforms were constantly checked to make sure the skirts were the right length, and you had the right socks, shoes, ties and sweaters on. I would sometimes sneak and wear my penny loafers, which got me a few demerits and detentions every time I got caught.

The classes were long and hard. The highlight of my day was Father Nelly's class. Father Nelly's class was for non-Catholic students who needed to learn about GOD. I learned a little in between starring at Father Nelly's baby blue eyes, dark brown curly hair and olive skin. I remember feeling guilty for being happy I was not Catholic so I could take his class. The second highlight of my day was the drill team that I had joined because that is what most of the black girls in the predominantly white school did. The captains were twins who were pretty and stylish even in their uniforms, and I liked them right away.

Everything was going well until I started hanging out with my old friends. They kept telling me how much fun they were having at the neighborhood school with all of our friends and family and I started to feel like I was missing out on something not being there. I did miss my old life, and all of my old friends at times, and I was always eager to hear all the gossip they had to share. I usually got a lot of laughs from the gossip that they told me, but I was starting to get comfortable at my new school, and I wanted to give it a chance. It was different from my normal life, but it was a really difficult adjustment.

One evening when I got home from school my cousins and sister were sitting on the porch talking to some boy on the telephone. We often met boys on the party line in the nineties. We would just pass the telephone around from person to person until we all got bored or fell asleep. I was always the last person to get home because my school was further away, and I usually had drill team practice. I guess during my absence is when my cousin and sister came up with the idea and thought it would be funny to hook me up with a guy that they had met through a friend of theirs because he was not attractive.

We started talking on the telephone every day after school until the wee hours of the morning, and eventually we set up a day to finally meet. My plan was to get a look at him while I was still on the bus and then decide if I was going to actually get off the bus and meet him. I do not know if he was used to girls not liking him after they saw him, or if my sister and cousin had tipped him off, because he was not at the bus stop when I arrived. I rode all the way from the other side of town to his neighborhood and he could not walk around the corner to the bus stop to meet me on time, this irritated me.

I decided to get off of the bus and call him from the pay phone to let him know that I had arrived. When he turned the corner and started walking towards me, I almost ran in the opposite direction. He looked like Harry from the movie Harry and the Henderson's. I instantly wanted to run, all I could think about at the time was punching my sister and cousin in the face for hooking me up with the boy. I sucked it up and did not run, besides, I was not ready to get on another bus to go home just yet, it had been a long ride over here.

He invited me to the house where he was staying at the time, and I accepted. I stayed there talking to him and trying not to stare at him for almost an hour. I only stayed an hour because I did not want to get home too late, and I was eager to cuss out my sister and cousin for pulling this little prank on me. As he was walking me to the bus stop all I could think of was getting away from him and never hearing from him again.

When I got home my sister and cousin was sitting on our porch. As soon as I reached the porch, I started yelling you bitches think that you are funny hooking me up with that big ugly boy! They just fell out laughing. I rolled my eyes at them and stormed off of the porch to go to my bedroom and start the mountain of homework that was due the next day. I was not interested in answering any of their questions. He tried calling me that night, but I just let the telephone ring hoping that he could take a hint. I felt like, we talked on the telephone for a while, we met, and now I was moving on to someone I was at least physically attracted to. I know it sounds harsh, but at fourteen-year-olds I did not have the skills to properly break up with somebody by just telling them.

I mean what was I supposed to say, I like talking to you, but I do not like the way you look so I cannot talk to you anymore. The next night he called me again and I did not answer, thank GOD for caller ID. Maybe a week or so later he called again, and my mother answered the telephone and told him I was home, and she handed me the phone. I took the phone and started talking to him, but I was cold and dry, and when he asked me where I had been, I got really defensive and he backed off.

I continued to talk to him, and after a few months he started to grow on me. I started to like him a little bit. I found out from talking to him that his older brothers were in the drug game and he was starting to take an interest in it. I did not realize how serious he was until about six months later when he started buying me expensive things like Gucci sneakers and pocketbooks, leather jackets, coats, jewelry, and he also gave me lots of money. I tried to hide most of the gifts he bought me from my family because I knew they would not be happy about me dating a drug dealer.

Back at school I was being called to the dean's office every month about my tuition not being paid. I saw that as my out. I told my mom that, if she could not afford the tuition at my catholic school to just transfer me to the neighborhood high school. She initially said no, until I just refused to go to school out of what I consider to be sheer rebellion. She eventually caved in and registered me at Germantown High School. This was one of the biggest mistakes of my life. I should have stayed put, but hindsight is twenty-twenty.

10

Trauma 6: Domestic Abuse

I CONTINUED MY relationship which got stronger now that we were attending the same high school. After a few months he started to show signs of jealousy and I did not like it. We began to argue a lot because I was not going to let him control me. The more I pulled away from him, the more he tried to control me. I would skip school to hang out with him, but that was not enough. He wanted me in his presence from the time I left my house in the morning until the time I went home in the evening. If I was not with him physically, I was on the telephone with him.

I finally got sick of it and decided I wanted to end the relationship because his jealousy was out of control. One night, I was at his grandmother's house visiting him when his jealousy reared its ugly head again. His older brothers and their friends stopped by and he was in another room when they got there. When he returned, he kept asking me if any of them had said anything to me. I told him numerous times that all they had said was hello and asked me if I was okay. As soon as they started drinking, it got worse. He started accusing me of lying to him, so I decided to leave.

I called my cousin to come and pick me up and that made him even angrier. Now he was drunk and angry, so I decided to gather my things and wait outside for my cousin. I got my belongings together and began walking down the stairs. He started following me out of the front door. I was standing on the front porch praying my cousin would hurry up and pull up.

As soon as he spotted her car, he snatched my coat out of my hands and told me that since he had bought it, he was keeping it. I said fine, I have other coats and I started walking down the stairs. Then he changed his mind and tried to give me the coat back, as I went to grab the coat from his hands, he let it go and it fell on the steps. It was a white coat, so that really pissed me off. As I bent over to pick up the coat, he kicked me in my butt so hard that it sent me and the coat flying down the stairs. I was afraid and in shock, I just got up and ran towards the car. My cousin wanted to get out and fight, but I stopped her and said lets just go, he is drunk.

Sadly, that is not when the relationship ended. I still spoke to him on the telephone, but I tried to avoid seeing him in person. This did not make him happy and I could tell he was drinking more. Since he had already gotten kicked out of school for poor attendance and being a bully, I felt safe in school as long as I did not run into him on my way in or out of the building.

After a few months had passed, he seemed different, nicer, happier. I thought maybe he quit drinking and wanted to be a better person. We would sit on my porch and talk and laugh for hours. The problem was, I had met someone else by then that I was really starting to like, and I wanted to end the relationship with him for good.

We were hanging out one night on my porch when he

asked me to take a ride with him. Against my better judgment I agreed, and we ended up at his mother's house. I reluctantly went inside the house, even though my intuition was screaming at me not to. He went upstairs and came back down a different person, he even looked like a different person in his face. He walked up to me with his face twisted up in anger and he grabbed me by the collar, he dragged me up the stairs to the bathroom and yanked down my pants, after he examined my underwear, and was satisfied by what he saw, he dragged me back down the stairs and into the kitchen. The next thing I know, he pulled out a gun and pointed it at me and demanded to know the name of the guy I had just started seeing. I was afraid and in shock, how did he find out that I was seeing someone else? He tricked me, he knew the whole time, that is why his attitude changed. He must have been stalking me and I did not even know it.

I had to think fast and figure out how to get the hell out of here in one piece. I started crying and telling him that I did not know who he was talking about, then I heard the gun cock. I dove under the kitchen table, but I kept my eyes on him. I had to tune out his yelling because I was trying to concentrate on not getting shot. Then it occurred to me, his mother was probably upstairs sleeping. His mother was a robust woman that always wore a scowl on her face and did not play any games or tolerate any foolishness, I was scared to death of the lady.

I took a deep breath, and then I yelled out, if you do not put that gun down, I'm going to scream for your mother. Before I could make good on my promise to scream, his mother appeared in the kitchen doorway. She started yelling and screaming at him and she told him to get out of her house. She told me that I needed to stay away from him, and that he had another girl pregnant. She was kind enough to give me cab fare to get home, and I never saw either one of them again.

I did not call the police or tell my mother when I got home, I just moved on with my life like it never happened. I justified it by telling myself that I should have known better than to go anywhere with his crazy drunk ass. In hindsight, I can see that it was the traumas that I had already been through, that allowed me to stay in this relationship after seeing the first few red flags. No amount of jewelry, Gucci, or money is worth staying in an abusive situation. These traumatic seeds that were planted early on in my life caused me to make decisions that caused me more traumas. It was a vicious cycle that went on for decades, one relationship after another, until I got sick of it and chose to just stay single.

11

Trauma 7: Teen Mom

By the time I had turned fifteen years old I was pregnant again. I had also gotten kicked out of my mother's house, so I dropped out of high school and I ended up in a juvenile detention center. One night after I snuck into my mother's house after curfew, she called the police and reported me for truancy. I guess she thought the scared straight route would do me some good. I can honestly admit that I was lost. In my mind, I had already handled so many adult responsibilities in my short life that I thought I was mature enough to make my own decisions about my life.

Being confined in a Juvenile detention center was an experience that I did not want, but I needed it at the time. It provided me with structure, discipline and time to think. I still had not told anyone else about my pregnancy, but I knew that the staff was going to find out from the blood I had to give during my intake. I was afraid because I knew they were going to tell my mother, I could not sneak off to planned parenthood this time, I was going to have a baby.

When I went to court the first time my mother did not show up, so I was sent back to the detention center and given a new court date two weeks away. I called her later that night to find out why she did not show up to my court hearing. The only explanation she gave me was, she had to work that day. When the detention center found out about my pregnancy, I was transferred to a different facility where they sent children that might pose some type of liability to the facility. The new place was a cabin style house in the woods that was for girls who had not been sentenced to any jail time yet.

These girls had committed crimes that I had never even heard of. Most of them had been through things in their short lives that no one should have had to experience. Getting to know these girls and listening to their life stores definitely helped me put things in my life into prospective. I knew I was heading in the wrong direction before I got here, and I needed to figure out what I was going to do after I got out of here. I had to prepare for the birth of my baby. It was scary to have this amount of responsibility at such a young age, but this was my reality.

Because my only charge was truancy and I was pregnant, the staff was kind of lenient on me. The house we lived in was comfortable, but Ms. Thomas our house mother was mean. She did not tolerate whispering or more than two girls hanging out together at a time. Our daily routine was, everyone was awakened at 6 a.m., we had breakfast, went to school, after school we had extracurricular activities, dinner, two hours of television time, shower time, and bed by 10 p.m.

When my next court date came, I was sure I was getting out of there. When I entered the court room, I saw my mother and I felt relieved. When they called my name, I stood up and listened while the judge spoke to my mother. The judge explained to her that since I had not committed a real crime that she could take me home and try and work things out. It sounded reasonable to me and the judge, but not to my mother. She told the judge that she did not want me at home, and that she wanted me to stay locked up until I turned eighteen. My bottom jaw hit the courtroom floor; I could not believe what she had just said.

The judge told her that, I had not committed a crime and that she would have to sign over her parental rights and make me a ward of the state in order for her to get rid of me. Since I still had not been charged with a crime or sentenced to any amount of time, I was scheduled to come back to court in two more weeks. I had been locked away for a little over a month, and I was feeling really homesick and abandoned. I would call my girlfriends and my grandmother when I was able to use the telephone just to feel normal. I had accepted the situation for what it was, and I tried to make the best of it since I was not going anywhere anytime soon.

By the time my third court date came up, I did not expect much because of what happened the last time. I looked around the room and I spotted my mother with tears in her eyes. I was confused, until I saw my grandmother sitting next to her. This time when the judge called my name, my grandmother stood up first. The judge asked her who she was, and she told him that she was my grandmother. The judge asked my mother again, was she ready to take me home.

Before she could answer, my grandmother said yes Judge we are going to take her home today. She looked at my mother who was still crying, and she just nodded her head in compliance. I was jumping up and down inside, I was finally going home. After the paperwork was signed, I quickly changed clothes, grabbed my belongings and walked out of the front door on my own, without handcuffs or a police officer for the first time in over two months. By the time we reached the car, my mother had stopped crying, but she was quiet. We dropped my grandmother off at her home and we drove the rest of the way to our house in silence.

When we arrived at home I noticed that not much had changed since I have been gone the last two and a half months. Things were a little awkward between me and my mother, but I was not really worried about that because I was too excited to be home. The first thing I did was take a long hot bath. The next thing I did was get my hair done, I had one of the girls I bunked with braid it in individual plats to protect it from breaking off. after that, I got dressed and headed out to see my friends and family. I was not ready to see my child's father just yet because I was not ready to deal with the drama of my pregnancy yet.

I was ordered by the court to return back to school or I would be put away again. I was enrolled in an alternative school for pregnant teens. The school was in an old church in West Philadelphia, it was dusty and dim and smelled of mil-dew. The best thing about the place was the hot lunches. The classes were short, and the schoolwork was elementary, but it was keeping me free, so I learned to love it.

About a week after my release, I had to muster up the strength and courage to deal with the father of my child. When I finally saw him, he told me that my cousins and my sister had already told him where I was, and that I was pregnant. He did not seem to upset that I had not contacted him while I was away or that I was pregnant. After we discussed the pregnancy and my experience of being locked up, we started to reconnect and rebuild our relationship. I had no idea what I was getting myself into at the time. I thought we were back together and building a life together, but what I did not know was that he had rekindled his relationship with his other baby's mother while I was away, and she was pregnant too.

Things never really got any better at home between my mother and I so I ended up moving in with my aunt so I could figure things out. My support group consisted of my friends, my baby's father and my aunt. My mother took me to the welfare office and applied for health insurance and food stamps for me and my baby. Now that I had a place to live, food, health insurance and emotional support, I could focus on giving birth in a few months. I had decided to take the GED test after the baby was born. Trying to find childcare for a newborn so I could return to high school for six or seven hours a day was going to cost money that I did not have.

It is hard to put the experience of childbirth into words. It is an indescribable pain that you can only relate to if you have experienced it. After all the agonizing pain and screaming, I had given birth to a beautiful baby girl that weighted eight pounds and seven ounces, with a head full of beautiful black curly hair. I could not believe that I had actually given birth to a child. I was afraid to hold her when the nurse tried to give her to me even though she was the size of a two-month-old baby instead of a newborn. I kept seeing the face of my first-born child every time I looked at her.

While I was in the hospital, I tried to act normal like I was excited about giving birth, but I was not. I was scared, confused, withdrawn and sad and I did not know why. I was not able to bond with my child due to the fear of the unknown and my own haunting thoughts. At sixteen years old I had no idea what post-partum depression was. No one asked me how I was feeling after giving birth, and I did not say anything, but my feelings and emotions started to manifest in my behavior.

I sunk deeper into a depression, I just wanted to run away from it all and hide. I started hanging out late at night, partying and drinking. I would sleep in late the next day and neglect my baby's needs. My family would step in and take care of my daughter a lot. It caused a lot of resentment and conflict amongst me and my family.

My child's father had another family and trying to get him to take care of us was a lost cause. His other children's mother and I did not respect each other's roles in his life, we could not stand each other. I honestly did not have a problem with her at first, but I felt like I had to defend myself and my daughter against her. I was more interested in partying and having fun than I was in fighting some chick who had three babies by my baby's father. He had already broken my heart into a million little pieces while I was pregnant, and I was ready to move on.

While I was stuck in the house pregnant, he took the liberty of running around with all the neighborhood girls. Most of them knew about me and his other family but they did not care. They knew he had money and had an everyman for themselves mentality. I had cried my last tear over him; I had my eye on someone else now. His sister would often tell me that if he caught me, he was going to want to fight me. I really did not care about his feelings by this time, and I was not afraid of him, so I started dating my crush behind his back.

One spring day my girlfriend and I were walking down the street when my daughters father and his other baby's mother pulled up in his car. I had had enough of this entire situation by this time, and I was tired of arguing with the both of them. She wanted him to make me and my child feel less important to him than her and her children, and I was over it. I swiftly handed my bags to my girlfriend and told her to step out of the car. She refused to get out of the car. She said, I do not want to fight you. I did not understand these two, why would you pull up on someone starting drama, if you did not want to fight? We had already exchanged words a few times and I did not want to hear anymore from either one of them.

I angrily grabbed my bags back from my girlfriend and continued walking to my destination. About a week or so later, I had left my daughter with his mother to go and run some errands with his sister who was a friend of mine. An hour or so after we left, my sister called me and said that she had received a telephone call from some girl saying that I had better come and pick up this "it."

The "it" she was referring to was my daughter. I raced back over to his mother's house, my sister and cousin were already waiting outside to pick up my daughter. His mother told me that it was my sister wife that had made the call not her. I took my daughter to my mother's house, but I knew in my heart that this was not over. I did not necessarily want a problem with her, but clearly, she was not going to just leave me alone.

The next time I saw her, I calmly told her that I did not have a problem with her, but that if she said anything else about my daughter, that I would kick her ass. This girl stood in my face and said, "if I called her an it, than she is an it." Before I could talk myself out of it, I had punched her so hard in her face, that I thought my hand was broken, and we started fighting. His sister would not allow anyone to break it up and that was all I needed.

She instructed everyone to let us fight it out and get it off of our chest. I opened up a can of whoop ass on that girl, I beat on her until I was tired and out of breath. Later that night, our baby's father called to ask me if it was necessary for me to beat her up that bad. I explained to him that, if they both did not stay away from me, they would get more of the same treatment. I was finally free of all the drama until I met my son's father. By the time I turned twenty years old, I had given birth to my second child and the cycle started all over again.

Right after my son's first birthday, I decided that I had to stop feeling sorry for myself and figure out how I was going to create a good healthy life for myself and my children. I went through a few state required welfare programs that did not lead to full time employment. One day my girlfriend and I went to our neighborhood bar to get a drink and enjoy the all you can eat crab legs special. The bartender that was working approached us and asks us if we were interested in learning how to bartend. We both said yes, and she told us to meet her back at the bar in a few days.

When that day arrived, I called my girlfriend, but she said that she could not make it because she did not have a babysitter for her son. I decided to go alone because bartending appeared to be an easy way to make money. When I arrived at the bar, I asked the bartender if Anna was there because she had asked me to meet her there. She said that Anna was not there, and that her name was Lacy, and that Anna had told her that two girls were coming in to be trained that evening. I told her that my girlfriend was not going to be able to make it, but that I was ready to be trained.

I went behind the bar and she handed me an apron, receipt book and a pen. I was a little confused, and I guess the confusion was written all over my face because Lacy said that I was going to start training in the kitchen first. I accepted it because I really needed the money, those welfare checks were just not enough to survive off of. I was going to be earning fifty dollars a day, and I would be working from Tuesday through Saturday, from 11 a.m. to 6 p.m., and the shift included one free meal. It worked for me, the bar was close to my apartment, my boss was friendly, fair, and funny and everyone loved him including me.

I worked in the kitchen handling all the food orders. The cooks quickly learned that I would give them hell if things did not run smoothly. I grew to enjoy the job; I knew most of the patrons that frequented the bar because I had grew-up and still lived in the same neighborhood. The only rule was that we had to watched Jerry Springer every day. We would shut off the jukebox and everyone had to be quiet unless they were talking about the show. It was a great atmosphere, it reminded me of the show Cheers.

After a few months of working in the kitchen, my boss asked me if he could speak to me after my shift was over. He told me that a lot of the patrons at the bar really liked me, and that he wanted to give me a shot at being a bartender. He explained that my hours would change from the day shift to the night shift, and that Lacy would train me. Lacy was a great bartender, she kept everything simple. I respected Lacy because she was not just a bartender, she was a real estate agent as well. She drove a nice car; she had her own place, she was classy, and had bigger goals and dreams, bartending was just a part of her hustle.

I borrowed Lacy's blueprint. I bartended in the evenings and worked a mirage of nine to five jobs in the daytime. I barely slept or ate, but I was beginning to see the light at the end of the tunnel. I followed this blueprint for almost five years. I was chasing an illusion of the life I thought I wanted so much, that I lost sight of the bigger picture, myself, my children and the direction my life was heading in. I eventually realized that I was in a rat race that was going nowhere besides in a circle. My children and I were not starving, but I had lost my focus by saying yes to any job that offered a paycheck.

I decided it might be time for me to formulate a new plan. I started to scale back on bartending and take back full custody of my children. They were in my cousin's custody while I worked and partied. By this time, I was twenty-four years old. I had a great reputation amongst the night life community, I was an excellent bartender, I did not do hard drugs, and I did not sleep with the customers. I started to only take jobs where there would be at least two hundred people or more attending. This way I could maximize what I made while only working half the time. I wanted to focus more on transitioning from bartending to a secure, stable job in the legal field, that was my passion.

I purchased a GED book and started studying for the test. I knew that was the first thing I needed to accomplish in order for me to get into college. I sacrificed the money I was missing out on and just focused on passing the test. I had about six months to prepare for the next test and I was determined to pass it. The day that I took the test I was relaxed because I knew I had studied, and I was prepared. I could only do my best at this point and hope for the best.

I arrived early on test day so that I could relax and drink a cup of coffee before the test. The campus looked like its own city inside of a city. I found a Dunkin Donuts on the campus and went inside. I ordered an extra-large coffee and found a comfortable sofa tucked in a corner. After I took the test, I felt really good about it. I felt as if I had accomplished something, I felt one step closer to my dreams.

I got my test scores a few week later and my hopefulness was crushed. I had passed four out of the five tests with great scores, but I had failed the math portion of the test. After a few weeks of self-loathing, I started studying the math test again. I retook the test a month later and I passed it. When I received the letter in the mail stating that I had passed the GED test, I danced around my bedroom until I was tired and out of breath. Now I could finally go to college!

It was a long steady climb transitioning from bartending to becoming a paralegal, but it was worth it. I loved school, and I knew I had chosen the correct field of study. Being a paralegal would be the first step, then getting a job and eventually law school. I believe I chose the legal field because I believed in justice and protecting the rights and liberties of people from injustices and I wanted to help. I loved being a paralegal, it was very fulfilling to my soul for the first eight years. By the ninth year I was burnt out, and I felt depleted. When my mother died, it was exactly the trauma I needed to wake me up and look at what I was doing wrong. I was not maximizing my life and living up to my full potential. I was giving too much of myself without replenishing myself.

Becoming a teen mom was a decision that plagued me with a lot of shame and guilt for a long time. I believed I was guilty of dragging two innocent children through my life's struggles, abandoning them during my dark times and not being able to give them the love, time and attention they deserved and needed to thrive as children. We were surviving not thriving, no one taught me how to thrive and that needed to be corrected. The shame I felt was constantly being reflected back to me by my family, friends, and society through gossip, judgement, and blame for getting pregnant at a young age in the first place. I got to a point where I thought to myself, why beat yourself up, society has got that part coved. I had to drop the defenses and just live my life, I wanted to thrive.

I believe we are all just teachers and mirrors for each other. We need to see ourselves through other people's actions or inactions in order to recognize, and change the things that we do not like about ourselves? If we could just put judgement on the back burner for just a moment, we would be able to relate to one another better by having empathy and compassion for each other's trials, tribulation, and traumas. Yes, I am guilty of judging people as well in the past, but when I learned better I did better. If you have a conscious, it feels wrong when you are doing it, or immediately afterward, but society has taught us that it is okay. Just because we have been judged and hurt does not give us the right to judge and hurt others.

I survived being a teen mom, rape, neglect, abuse, abandonment, backstabbing, you name it, I have probably experienced it, and overcame it, and so can you. It was a journey of ups and downs, filled with mistakes, regrets, and a lot of learning about myself, my children, family, and the way society is structured. I also discovered that I am strong, resilient, and capable of creating the life of my dreams by identifying and following my purpose. I am the master of my own destiny. Once I understood that, and accepted my life's purpose, I took flight, eager to see what the next chapter of my life held.

I never knew what self-love was, or that it even existed until I decided to say yes to this journey. Now that I have it, it has transformed me into a new person. I have learned and developed some of my own tools to transform my life of trauma into a trauma free life that is filled with compassion, empathy, respect, understanding, and forgiveness, for myself first, and to all of humanity because we all need to heal from one trauma or another. I understand that we are all one, and we need each other's help as mirrors on our journeys to self-discovery and self-love. Now when issues arise in my life, I deal with them in a manner that is beneficial for all parties involved. I want everyone to walk away from the situation feeling heard, loved, and understood.

I went through a lot in the first thirty years of my life. I had a ten-piece set of luggage full of traumas to unpack when I first started this journey. I experienced every emotion known to man, but this time around I had to learn how to sit with it. I had to feel it; I had to talk to my traumas and ask them questions.

Once I understood it, I could forgive myself and all parties involved and release it from my soul. Releasing traumas works just like forgiveness. It does not require involving anyone else, or even rekindling a relationship with anyone. It is just accepting what has happened, understanding who should be held accountable and making peace with the truth.

If you are responsible for causing trauma to yourself or someone else, you must forgive yourself as well. We are all capable of making the wrong the choices and decisions. Sometimes these decisions land us in a negative or traumatic situation, but these situations are just lessons for us to learn from. I cannot blame anyone else for going to a boy's house after being warned by my intuition not to. What he did to me was not my fault, but I had to take accountability for my actions.

Going within, in deep mediation allows us to access those traumas we have stored in there. I was able to breakdown the outer layer of the walls that I built up to protect myself in therapy. By talking and being willing to open up, I was able to see I was no different than anyone else that was willing to be honest about their life's struggles. I had no reason to be ashamed of anything I had been through or done in my life. Through therapy I learned how to feel again. I learned that my emotions were not dangerous, but the way I expressed them could be.

When I started to unpack all the clutter, the confusion stopped, the fog floated out of my life and the clarity I was looking for came rushing in. It was the total opposite of what I was experiencing before I decided to go to therapy. Before therapy, my mind was in a fog, I could not think straight, eat, or sleep. With a clear mind, I could just focus on healing. I can promise you that if you sit in your pain, and work through it, you will not explode into a million pieces and die. You will actually be taking the first step toward healing and living, not just existing.

When you stop existing and start living your entire perspective of life changes. By clearing the clutter within, you are able to reconnect with your true authentic self. The self you were before those traumas happened. Before you felt like you were forced to put up walls and wear a mask to hide who you truly are from the world to protect yourself from being hurt. If you go within and face your traumas, heal them, and release them, you will no longer be triggered by it. For instance, if one of your triggers are jealousy, go within and explore that. Ask yourself, why I am jealous of this person and why do I believe that they have something that I am not capable of having?

When the answers to your questions arrive, it will probably shock you where the traumas originated from. I was, but after I examined it, and understood it, I was able to let it go with love, understanding and forgiveness for myself. Now I am able to be happy for someone else's accomplishments or good fortune without comparing them to mine. That trigger has now been removed from your soul. Our emotions can be just like newborn babies. They need to be nurtured so we can master them and control them, not become a slave to them. There are people that believe that by controlling someone else, they are in control of themselves and their own emotions, but this is false. If you feel the need to control other people, then you have already lost control of yourself. You have given away your power to something or someone outside of yourself. We consciously or unconsciously do this and then wonder why it all fell apart.

I have learned to live from within, by going within and cleaning house so I would be comfortable living there. I had to get rid of the clutter, sort through everything and get rid of what I no longer needed to survive because I was no longer trying to survive. Once your house is clean, neat and organized, you can start to rebuild your foundation. A foundation built on love, honesty, self-respect, boundaries, and balance for yourself and others.

Having healthy boundaries and enforcing them will keep you from being used, disrespected, and taken for granted. Boundaries will require you to put yourself first, and also make sure that you will do what is best for yourself without feeling guilt or shame. Enforcing boundaries is not easy if you were once a people pleaser or codependent because if someone or something violates your boundaries, you will have to be strong enough to walk away from it. Would you pick up an old dirty broken couch from the sidewalk and bring it into your nice new home to sit on? No, you would not, you would leave it exactly where you found it and keep walking. This is how you will begin to view anything that tries to cross a boundary. leave it on the curb!

When you learn to love yourself, you are not just going to accept whatever is being offered to you without examining it and deciding if you want it or need it. These decisions will be difficult to master in the beginning, but it gets easier, the more you learn to love yourself. This journey is not a marathon, take your time and do not rush the process. Sometimes you may have to unplug and just smell the roses, or get some rest, or change your diet, it going to be different for everyone. Whatever it is, if it does not come from within, it is probably not the best decision for you. Your spirit is always guiding you, but you will need a clear channel to connect to it and receive the messages.

Even after you master living from within, there will be times when you will make the best decision for yourself, and you receive positive results from that decision. When that happens, you have to congratulate yourself on a job well done, instead of beating yourself up and feeling guilty that you disappointed someone else. Making these decisions and sticking to your guns is not always easy to do. There are no longer the feelings or emotions of blame, shame, guilt, regret, or embarrassment for yourself or anyone else. All those emotions are replaced with love, compassion, oneness, and understanding for humanity. My universal prayer is that people wake up to who they truly are and how their decisions may affect someone else. We all have something to learn, teach, and overcome.

You will no longer make decisions from a broken place, or your ego. You will not need to get revenge or hold grudges, because you know it is not beneficial to you or your spiritual growth. Instead, go within where you can dissect the situation, understand your role, find the lesson, and release it with love and understanding. There is something within that is causing you to have this experience, and the only way to find out what it is, is to go within and ask yourself. Your higher self always knows, do not doubt it, or dismiss it when it reveals itself.

Go deeper, ask it some questions and trust the feedback it gives you even if makes you uncomfortable. It is the fear of these traumas that keep us stuck replaying the trauma over and over. That will keep happening until you acknowledge it and heal it. It is like a young child that needs some attention. They will do anything they can to get your attention. Some children act out negatively, and some positively.

Acting out positively can be people pleasing and wanting to be liked by everyone. When my masked started to crack and fall off of my face, I started to act out negatively. I did not have a healthy balance over my emotions. I gave other people the power to control my emotions because I thought I needed them in my life for one reason or another. When I started to understand that I had everything I needed within, I was able to take my power back and I stopped caring if someone liked me or not. As long as I was being authentic, and true to myself and my personal beliefs, it became easier for me to walk away from unauthentic relationships.

Being wrapped up in a bunch of unauthentic relationships is exhausting. Eventually the mask will start to suffocate you and kill your spirit, or someone will rip it off. I would suggest removing it yourself and dealing with what caused you to wear it in the first place. If you do not do the work from within, you will eventually put the mask back on. I have done this also, what I learned is that, the lessons got harder and the consequences were greater. When I finally got tired of being on an emotional rollercoaster ride, I made the decision to do the healing work that was necessary and threw the mask in the trash where it belongs.

The healing work is a big commitment. You are making a commitment to heal yourself and be the best person you can be. We commit to employers, gyms, and housing, but not to ourselves. I believe we do this unconsciously because we were never taught how to commit and love ourselves from the inside out. Other people may come along to lend you a hand from time to time, but ultimately you have to save yourself.

When I finally understood this truth, I was no longer looking for a person or a job to save me. If you put another person, place or thing on a pedestal, you are left devastated when it does not work out the way you expected it to. When I did not get the promotion at work, I let it turn my life upside down. I could have just accepted it, found another job and moved on, but I did not possess the tools at the time. Instead, I let my ego take over and lead me down a rabbit hole of self-destruction.

Final Words

AS I PACK my spiritual bags preparing for ascension, I look around at my surroundings with a slight smile on my face, thinking wow, I spent forty years in this matrix thinking that it was real, and calling it life. I was unaware that I was being duped and controlled by society this entire time. It was a hard pill to swallow, but I could not get stuck here, I had to keep going. Conscious living or awaking to what is really going on in the world is not for the faint of hearts. Ignorance is bliss, but it also robs you of the life you were meant to live and the person you were meant to be.

I tried to drag a few people with me, but I quickly learned that, this is my journey, they have their own journeys and I could not take them with me, nor could I go with them. I could be there for support, and encouragement, but I could not go within them and fix anything. I had to keep walking alone for now. Whoever or whatever is still there when I get to the next chapter of my life, is what was meant to be there to assist me in getting to the next level of consciousness.

The reality I was accustomed to no longer exist; I did not

believe in it anymore. It was time for me to co-create the life I wanted with the Divine and my authentic self. One that is consciously made, not one created out of fear, desperation, or survival. I know that I am bigger than any fear or obstacle. My choice to ascend in consciousness and being self-aware was by far one of the best moves I have ever made. Now that I am free, I want to assist others in breaking free and beginning their journeys of self-discovery.

Humanity has neglected their souls and ignored their spirituality, and I would like to see that change for all of our sake. People have adopted the corrupt ideals of society without questioning whether they are true and accurate and also if they are beneficial to humanity as a whole. We are existing and dying as if our lives have no real meaning and nothing could be further from the truth. It is painful to watch without wanting to save people from themselves, but you know what they say, when the student is ready the teacher will appear. All of my teachers have shown up on time to teach me what I needed to learn to get to the next level of consciousness and spiritual growth and so will yours. What is your deepest fear? Are you ready to conquer it?

"Our Deepest Fear"

"Our deepest fear is not that we are inadequate. Our deepest fear is that we are powerful beyond measure. It is our light, not our darkness that most frightens us, We ask ourselves, Who am I to be brilliant, gorgeous, talented, and fabulous? Actually, who are you not to be? You are a child of God. Your playing small does not serve the world. There is nothing enlightened about shrinking so that other people won't feel insecure around you. We are all meant to shine as children do. We were born to make manifest the glory of God that is within us. It's not just in some of us; it's in everyone. And as we let or own light shine, we unconsciously give other people permission to do the same. As we are liberated from our own fear, our presence automatically liberates others."

By Marianne Williamson

Trauma Self-Assessment Questionnaire

Please answer the below self-assessment questions as honestly as you can. These questions will help you identify your traumas and other things in your life you would like to change, work on, and heal.

1. Did you have a happy childhood?
2. Did you feel loved as a child?
3. Was love expressed to you by actions or words as a child?
4. Did you experience any traumas when you were a child?
5. Were your traumas acknowledged and validated by your family after you told them about them?
6. Did you receive any type of help or support to deal with your traumas?
7. Do you often think about your traumas?
8. What triggers you to think about your traumas?
9. How do you respond when one of your traumas are triggered?
10. Are you easily angered when triggered?
11. Has your traumas caused you any setbacks in your life?
12. Do your traumas cause you to suffer from anxiety?

13. Have you ever had an anxiety or panic attack?

14. Have you ever been diagnosed with having a mental illness?

15. Do you believe you are mentally ill?

16. Do you think your life would be more fulfilling if you no longer had traumas living within?

17. How would your life be different if you healed your traumas?

18. Are you willing to attend therapy sessions?

19. Do you feel like all of your traumas are someone else's fault?

20. Are you ready and willing to do the work to heal your traumas?

CPSIA information can be obtained
at www.ICGtesting.com
Printed in the USA
LVHW042343121020
668648LV00003B/222